25 YEARS OF
mac

The Best of MAC's Cartoons
from the *Daily Mail*, 1971-96

Stan McMurtry mac

Edited by Mark Bryant

Park McDonald
London

**For Nick and Mary, Maureen, Karen, Andy,
my wife Janet, my mother, sisters and Glyn**

First published in 1996 by Park McDonald

Park McDonald is an imprint of Deirdre McDonald Books
7 Westhorpe Rd, London SW15 1QH

ISBN 1 898094 17 9

Printed and bound in Great Britain by
BPC Consumer Books Ltd

INTRODUCTION

This year the *Daily Mail* celebrates its 100th birthday and I find myself with two conflicting emotions. Firstly, a sense of pride that I have been part of such a great newspaper for so long, and second, a feeling of disbelief that during its century of publication it has been employing me for a quarter of it. Twenty-five years! Where has it all gone? It seems such a short time ago since I walked through the entrance of Northcliffe House in London's Tudor Street, nervously clutching my drawing-pad and a brief-case containing some sandwiches, a few pencils and a good-luck card from my wife and children. I had been given a tiny little office on top of the building well away from the bustle and thrum of the main editorial floor. From its window I could see a tower with a large clock on one wall, the hands of which seemed to travel at an alarming rate as I struggled for ideas to take down to the Editor.

I had only been taken on to the paper for a trial period and was so unsure of myself and determined to please that I would submit between 15 and 20 rough ideas each day which, looking back, must have been a terrible ordeal for my poor Editor. Nowadays I'm not usually in quite such a panic and restrict myself to about five roughs every morning.

It was in the same small Tudor Street office a few years later that the equipment on my desk suddenly jumped several inches, spilling ink and pencils everywhere. This was followed by a dull thud and, looking up, I saw a plume of smoke rising from between the buildings opposite. This was the Old Bailey bomb planted by the IRA.

Most editorial cartoonists have been compelled to draw serious cartoons commenting about the atrocities perpetrated by the IRA in Northern Ireland and here on the mainland. A problem which frequently arises when making a serious political comment is that some readers turn to the cartoon page expecting a funny idea and assume wrongly that the artist is trying to make a joke out of an appalling situation. Consequently we get floods of complaining letters and occasionally a threatening one purporting to come from the IRA but which, I suspect, is more likely to be from a reader in need of a good psychiatrist.

Today , 7 January 1961

After years of sending drawings to the press, this was the first cartoon I ever had published. I remember the incredible elation I felt after opening the envelope and finding I'd got my first acceptance. It was to be several months before I got my second.

'Your wife just rang, Comrade Minister – don't forget to buy some carrots and potatoes for dinner...' *4 May 1971*

Here is the very first MAC cartoon that was published in the Daily Mail. *Looking at the crudity of the drawing today, I'm surprised it wasn't my last!*

Luckily the job I do doesn't always mean staring at a blank piece of paper praying for inspiration to come in an office. A year after joining the *Daily Mail* I was fortunate enough to travel with a few other British cartoonists to the USA where we were guests of the American Cartoonists' Association. At their convention we were looked after right royally by a wonderfully hospitable bunch of Americans who were conducting a series of scientific tests to see how much Jack Daniel's whiskey a British cartoonist could hold before falling over.

The highlight of the week was to be a grand dinner which would be attended by the President of the United States himself.

So hospitable were the Americans that often it was difficult to meet the daily deadline at which time I had to send a pungent comment on the day's happenings down what was then called 'The Line' (an early steam-driven fax machine fed with coal from the front) to my London office. These drawings were executed (an apt word) on my hotel-room table, so while everyone else was out sightseeing and enjoying themselves, I had my nose pressed firmly to a hot sketch-pad. Later, when my children asked: 'What's America like, Daddy?' I was able to describe in detail one hotel bedroom, two bars in 42nd Street and a convention centre in Washington.

Sadly, due to unforeseen business, the President was unable to join us for dinner after all, so I didn't get to meet him. I learned later that President Nixon was busy at a place called 'Watergate' at the time...

Another little excursion from the office was when I was sent to present the original of a cartoon which had been requested by a nudist colony near Orpington. This was another convention and nudists from several different countries were there in several different shapes and sizes. The Editor had had the bright idea of sending me, plus a photographer, to hand over the drawing personally. This involved stripping off and posing beside two nude ladies

with the cartoon discreetly covering my private bits. However, the photographer, being a friendly soul, had plans to pin full-frontal MAC photos all round the office on our return, so before he could take his lens cap off, I had my underpants back on!

As far as politics go, I suspect that most people in my profession would prefer it if there was a law which would make all people with bland or uninteresting faces ineligible for office. Most of us would vote in politicians with big ears, misshapen noses and bald heads, preferably with a few warts, bandy legs and buck teeth. They are easier to draw and make the whole business of caricature so much simpler. John Major, for instance, with his grey hair parted on the right, glasses and protruding upper lip is much easier to draw than Tony Blair who is younger, fairly unlined and devoid of any outstanding facial features. Luckily for us, the British voter has chosen to elect a good run of drawable prime ministers. Sir Alec Douglas-Home was wonderfully easy with his skull-like features, as was Sailor Ted Heath who was thick-set, had a distinctive hair-style and a florid complexion. Harold Wilson with his baggy eyes and his pipe was a gift, and Mrs Thatcher with her lacquered hair and severe expression could have stayed on for ever as far as most cartoonists were concerned.

Mrs Thatcher's reputation for being the Iron Lady gave me, and probably a lot of other people, the impression that she was large in stature too, so it was a big surprise when my wife and I were invited to 10 Downing Street to meet and shake hands with the diminutive lady who was running the country. In fact, as we stood sipping drinks with the other guests in a reception room, a good half an hour after shaking the hand which was controlling all our destinies, my wife whispered to me from the side of her mouth: 'When do we get to meet Mrs T?' I think she thought the lady who had greeted us at the door was the cleaner!

However, standing next to the Iron Lady on that occasion was the person whom I, and I'm sure most of my colleagues, miss most – Denis Thatcher. Denis, who put up with all our jokes about his golf and legendary prowess with a gin bottle with great humour, must be a remarkable man, for as far as I know, during all the years his wife was in office he never complained once about being the butt of the country's cartoon humour. Mark Thatcher had his moments, too, but we poked fun at him for entirely different reasons and never felt for him the warmth and high regard we had for his father. Besides, it seemed that Mark spent a lot of the Thatcher years being 'Lost'.

About sixteen years ago, for a bit of fun, I drew my wife Janet into the background of one of my cartoons, then later included her every day. Sometimes she would be in a shopping queue, the next day in the pattern of some curtains, perhaps in a picture hanging on a wall, and so on. Eventually I started to receive readers' letters asking who the mysterious blonde was, so, realizing that she had become a popular feature of the cartoon, I've drawn her in ever since. She only fails to appear on those days when I produce a serious cartoon with a heavy social or political comment. On a normal day, however, if I leave her out by mistake, not only do I get letters of complaint, I also don't get any breakfast!

On those rare breakfastless occasions I think perhaps I could persuade the Royal Army Catering Corps to rustle up a plate of bacon and eggs for me. Let me say now that the RACC are a unit of fit and active men. They are slim, trim and muscular and not at all like I

"I take it Egon Ronay has gone then?" *6 November 1984*

into position beneath the sweat, determined to show that anything an 18-year-old squaddie could do, so could I. Over the ditches we raced, vaulting the hurdles and clambering up the high rope walls.

Twenty of us running.

Nineteen hearts beating: Kaboom, Kaboom, Kaboom…

One heart beating: Shlurp, Shlurp, Shlurp…

Not that I was aware of it at the time. I was invincible, wasn't I?

Well, no. Two weeks later I was in hospital and off work for three months. OK, yes, I know I'm stupid trying to keep up with 18-year-olds. All right, yes, I've learned my lesson. But three months and no MAC cartoon! Did anybody notice it was missing? Did the circulation of the paper go up? I don't know, I didn't check.

I missed me! I missed doing the daily drawing. I enjoy it and if I can avoid any future challenges like going 10 rounds with Mike Tyson or being Arnold Schwarzenegger's stunt-man for a month, I hope to be drawing for some time to come.

I do hope you'll enjoy looking through this book and going back with me over the past 25 years. I'm looking forward to the next 25. Oh, and incidentally, I'm still waiting to hear whether I've got the job!

portrayed them in a cartoon soon after a story had appeared in the *Daily Mail* about Egon Ronay paying their camp a visit. In my drawing the cooks were as I remembered them from my National Service days: scruffy, spotty, and very fat. This drawing had so enraged the present purveyors of military cuisine that they threw down the gauntlet – or in this case perhaps we should call it an oven-glove – which took the form of a challenge to take part in their daily routine in the gymnasium and over the assault course. 'No problem,' I said.

Accompanied by a photographer, whose idea of a good work-out was lifting his camera to his eye or perhaps grinding out a cigarette with his heel, I joined the RACC trainees and hauled myself up ropes, tossed weights in the air, knocked off a few hundred press-ups and then jogged onto the assault course, a nonchalant expression fixed

CONTENTS

**THE
LONG ARM
OF THE
LAW**

A scheme was mooted in Parliament to ease traffic congestion in cities by
introducing still tougher parking restrictions for the poor motorist. Oh, how easy
they had it back then in 1973 – look at it now!

'...and if you haven't moved the bits in two minutes we get really nasty!' *20 January 1973*

There was uproar in the Sikh community when it was announced that crash helmets for motorcyclists were to be made compulsory. But it seemed that they might have ways of getting round it...

'And we can't do a damned thing – the driver's wearing a crash helmet!' *17 April 1978*

This was a gem of a story – the Government relaxed the law on 'red light' windows. Some cartoons almost seem to draw themselves...

'Doris! For Heaven's sake come away from that window!' *6 February 1976*

A lady named Joyce McKinney tied to a bed and then seduced a Mormon gentleman who wasn't keen on that sort of thing. She claimed in court that she would gladly ski naked down Everest for him with a rose stuck up her nose. Brrrr!

'I think it must be a police trap for Joyce McKinney.' *17 April 1978*

Another of my favourites from 1978, which needs no explanation.

'I think it's something to do with the sweeping new powers the police have asked for.'
4 August 1978

The 'Lucan Flying Circus' took off again when the fugitive earl was reputedly
spotted in South America.

15

'Good news, Lucan, old man – they're still searching for you down in Venezuela.'
13 September 1982

Canute had tried it and failed – but now it worked! Engineers turned the tide as the newly opened Flood Barrier stopped Old Father Thames rolling along.

'Oy! Do you know how much those gates going up and down costs?' *9 November 1982*

It was revealed that amongst the clients at the 'luncheon voucher' orgies held by Streatham's 'Madame Cyn', Cynthia Payne, were some senior police officers.

'I don't care where you're going later, Perkins! Get into uniform!' *13 February 1987*

'At this point, Hawkins, you explain to the gentleman there's an amnesty for drunken drivers and say how awfully pleased we'd be if he'd come back to our hospitality room for a cup of coffee.' *7 March 1988*

The notorious Hole-in-the-Wall ram-raiders gang struck for the fifth time over the holiday weekend, using a stolen JCB to scoop an Abbey National cash machine containing £55,000 at Hempstead in Kent.

'I told you not to stop at the lights!' *21 April 1992*

20 After a former London music-teacher was stabbed to death giving chase to a
vandal slashing car tyres, his killer's acquittal on a plea of self-defence seemed to
many the height of injustice.

Home Secretary Michael Howard called for 'vigilance, not vigilantes' as a Gallup survey revealed that public confidence in the police was at such a low ebb that 76% of those polled could consider becoming vigilantes.

'I do hope this doesn't mean an end to your valuable work for Neighbourhood Watch, Miss Penthrope...'

11 August 1993

22 Constable Richard King was convicted of assault and fined £150 when he punched a teenage passenger who allegedly threatened to throw his nine-week-old baby girl out of a train window.

'Sorry to trouble you, sir, but you appear to have thrown my family out of the window. Would you care to accompany me to the police station where we can discuss the matter over a cup of tea?' *9 March 1995*

**IN
SICKNESS
AND IN
HEALTH**

24 I'd forgotten all about this one until I saw a rather tatty cutting of it on an undertaker's office wall recently. Which just goes to prove that even in their rather solemn business the men in black hats have a sense of humour.

My missus would've won that title hands down if your flamin' cat hadn't got her!' *2 September 1971*

In order not to waste the time of doctors and nurses, hospital switchboard-operators were told to ascertain the urgency of calls. Nowadays perhaps one wouldn't even get the advice about aspirins...

The switchboard operator at the hospital says take two aspirins and stop wasting her time.'
10 March 1978

Medical history was made when a research scientist managed to successfully clone a frog. Future possibilities made the mind boggle...

'Daddy has warned you, Bernard – if you don't stop, he'll take your chemistry set away.'
27 July 1978

In a story that gripped the country, two distraught mothers waited anxiously for the answer to a nightmare question – had they taken the wrong babies home from the maternity hospital?

'Remember me? Next bed 16 years ago in the maternity hospital? – well it appears there was a mix-up with our babies...' *1 September 1986*

28   Four Turkish kidney-donors at the centre of the 'organs-for-sale' racket faced
criminal charges and four-year jail sentences following a national outcry over the
scandal of donors who were paid to travel to London for transplant operations.

'We only meant to sell one kidney but the children's school fees went up, then I needed new golf clubs, then...'

27 January 1989

'We've kept to your instructions, Prime Minister – that one's going to be a Labour supporter...' *24 April 1990*

30   I don't think I would have drawn this cartoon today, but in 1990 no one could have forecast that an illness in cattle would be linked to humans and cause the huge divisions in the EU that occurred six years later.

'It's not as bad as I feared – she's only got "extremely silly cow disease".' *15 May 1990*

Former US Army paramedic, Matthew Brafman, 33, was jailed for three-and-a-half years after the discovery that he had treated 440 patients in an Essex hospital without proper medical qualifications, his records having been forged.

'Bad news from the hospital, I'm afraid, Mr Penthrope – they suspect your hip operation was done by a bogus doctor.' *8 October 1992*

32 A blue budgerigar called Peter owned by 81-year-old Eileen Wilson of South Bank, near Middlesbrough – who had smoked 40 cigarettes a day for 64 years – was reported as the first bird victim of lung cancer by passive smoking.

'Honestly, Doctor, I'm trying to kick the habit – I'm down to ten budgies a week.' *28 January 1994*

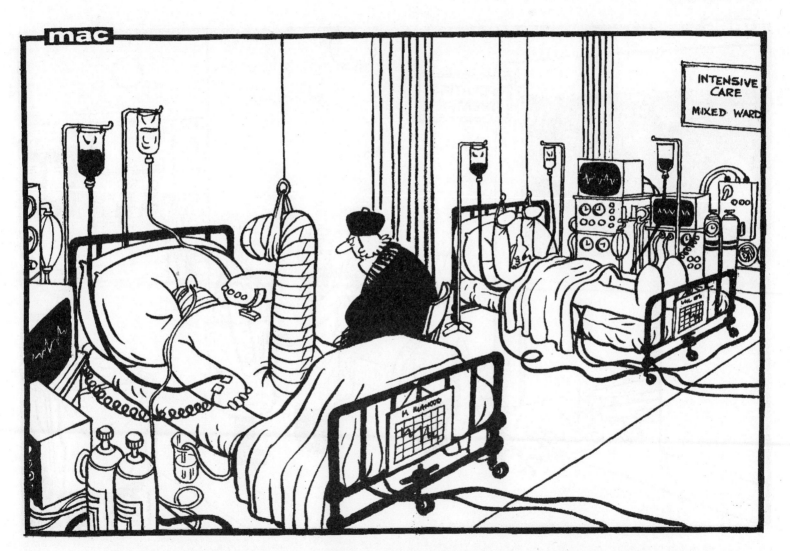

'I hope you're not getting up to anything with that woman in the next bed.' *24 November 1994*

34   A surgeon in a Cornish hospital was put on paid leave during an official inquiry
into allegations that he had allowed an operating-theatre nurse to remove a
patient's appendix.

**'NO, NO! How many times do I have to tell you, nurse?
The appendix is a small pink thing about this big...'** *13 January 1995*

In another surgical malpractice case it was revealed that a medically untrained hospital porter in Plaistow had been asked by a nursing sister to help out in a hip-replacement operation on a 71-year-old woman.

'Hang on, porter, we do hip replacements in the operating theatre...' *21 March 1995*

36 Health Secretary, Virginia Bottomley, was heavily censured by senior Tories as lacking 'moral courage' for surreptitiously announcing the closure of London hospitals in a Commons written reply instead of an open statement.

'While you were under the anaesthetic, Virginia Bottomley closed the hospital and sold it to Safeway.'

6 April 1995

THE ROYAL FAMILY

'...then when one discovers the mirror within oneself reflecting the fundamental meaning of life, one...'
23 September 1986

'Harry's great. But I feel Detective-Sergeant Throgmorton isn't terribly convincing as the Child in the Manger.'
8 December 1988

40   The Prince and Princess of Wales visited Hungary. Prince Charles, who had been
tutored in painting by Sir Hugh Casson, had many admirers of his watercolours.

'For Heaven's sake, Ludmilla! He hasn't got his art materials with him!' *8 May 1990*

A paternity suit filed in New Zealand against Captain Mark Phillips, estranged husband of the Princess Royal, caused considerable upset at Buckingham Palace.

41

'Frankly, Mother, we feel you're worrying too much about any fresh scandals hitting the family.'

26 March 1991

Eight-year-old Prince William started school at £2,350-a-term Ludgrove prep in Berkshire accompanied by a 'guardian angel' from Scotland Yard.

'Dammit, Sergeant Wilkins! We're supposed to be inconspicuous. Put out that ruddy pipe!'
11 September 1991

The Princess of Wales broke with tradition to become the first member of the Royal Family to own a foreign car, a metallic-red 157mph Mercedes-Benz 500SL.

'This'll put the cat amongst the pigeons – the Queen Mother buying a Harley-Davidson...' *6 February 1992*

44 Five months after the separation of the Duke and Duchess of York, the *Daily Mirror* published photographs of Fergie topless in the arms of her tax consultant, Texan millionaire John Bryan, on holiday in St Tropez.

'Look, Grandma – there's a girl over there getting financial advice.' *20 August 1992*

A book by the Duchess of York's friend, Lesley Player, revealed that the 34-year-old polo-player had had an affair with the Duchess's father, 61-year-old Major Ronald Ferguson. (Lots of complaints flooded in after this cartoon was published – it appears to be acceptable for reporters to write about such things, but not a subject for cartoonists to consider.)

'Promise me, darling. This will be our little secret.' *9 February 1993*

46 Leaked extracts from a book by *Daily Mirror* journalist, James Whitaker, claimed that MI5 had bugged the Prince of Wales's residence at Highgrove and recorded arguments between him and Princess Diana.

'...anyway, darlingest one. Check the house thoroughly. The thing you're looking for could be the size of a shirt button...' *14 May 1993*

Prince Charles's back problems returned when he suffered a bad fall during a polo match between the Prince of Wales's Maple Leaves and the Guards' Polo Club at Smith's Lawn, Windsor.

'Well, I finally did it, Mother – I had those troublesome vertebrae removed.' *15 June 1993*

48 *Princess in Love*, a kiss-and-tell romanticized account of the relationship between former cavalry officer Major James Hewitt and the Princess of Wales, was published to a storm of controversy.

'...with one bound I was by Queen Victoria's side, ripping the thin silk from...' *3 October 1994*

'. . . Anyway, there were three of us in the marriage, I became very sick, my husband didn't seem to care, so . . .' *4 December 1995*

50 Various members of the Royal Family have asked for the originals of my cartoons over the years, but I was especially pleased to have a request for this one from Her Majesty the Queen when security was tightened dramatically in 1996.

'I feel sorry for the corgis.' *27 February 1996*

RELIGIOUS MATTERS

'Well, shucks, if you were new to Arizona would you want to be cooped up in a darned Popemobile all day?'
14 September 1987

Churches were ordered not to give sanctuary to fugitives from justice. Home Secretary Douglas Hurd spoke out after immigration officers raided a Manchester church and seized a Sri Lankan trying to avoid deportation.

'I'm afraid I'm the bearer of some rather bad news, Lord Lucan...' *20 January 1989*

'First it became unsafe to have cigarettes, then sex, then food, then water – so I thought, what's left?'
10 February 1989

Islamic Fundamentalist leader, Ayatollah Khomeini, died without repealing his *fatwah* on Salman Rushdie, British author of the novel *The Satanic Verses* deemed blasphemous in Iran. I got a few sinister and rather threatening letters after this one appeared. Should I join Salman in hiding? What a thought! I decided I'd risk it and just locked my door.

5 June 1989

56 In London, twenty-five nuns organized a sponsored snooker tournament in order to raise money for their convent. (I got a lot of letters from snooker-players about this cartoon – pointing out that snooker-tables have eight legs...)

'Aw, c'mon, Sister Agatha. Stop messing about. Play fair!' *16 November 1989*

The authorities banned a Muslim film showing *Satanic Verses* author Salman Rushdie shooting and abusing Muslims before being struck dead by a bolt of lightning. It was later released on video.

'Excuse me – could you spare a little tomato ketchup?' *24 July 1990*

58 The Church of England's House of Bishops ruled that homosexual partnerships
amongst the clergy were permissible provided they remained celibate.

'...and do you, Eric of the gorgeous eyes and cute dimples, take Susan to be your lawful wife – or would you
like to change your mind?' *5 December 1991*

Despite a 20-year campaign for the acceptance of women priests, 40% of lay members opposed the motion at a meeting of the General Synod of the Church of England which requires a two-thirds majority for reforms.

'Y'know, Maisie – if they don't make up their minds soon about women priests, I'm going to have to consider something else...' *13 July 1992*

60 Following disastrous property speculation by the Church Commissioners resulting in losses of £800 million, the Archbishop of Canterbury announced cuts of £12 million to the salaries of Church of England clergy.

'Ah, here comes Gerald now. He's been out visiting the poor.' *17 February 1994*

Angela Berners-Wilson became the Church of England's first woman priest since the movement was founded by Henry VIII 460 years ago, when she and 31 others were ordained in Bristol Cathedral. This drawing upset the *Mail's* feminist readers – how dare I portray women priests as mindless chatterboxes! There were so many letters of complaint I very nearly did join Salman Rushdie in hiding.

'So anyway, Lord, I said to her, I said, "You're not really going to wear that hat with that dress are you?"
Well, she scowled at me and, honestly, Lord, if looks could kill ... anyway as I was saying ...' *14 March 1994*

27-year-old singer and former topless Page Three model, Samantha Fox, who had recently converted to Christianity, appeared before a crowd of 20,000 at the 21st Greenbelt Festival in Northamptonshire.

'Samantha Fox may have packed them in at the Christian pop festival, Miss Cheevly. But I think here at St Edmund's we'll stick to our traditional service.' *30 August 1994*

THE ENVIRONMENT

After weeks of drought in one of the hottest summers ever, the country was suddenly deluged with water, yet it was still a long time before water restrictions were lifted.

'You can't miss it – the standpipe is just at the foot of that lamp-post.' *27 September 1976*

To combat the water crisis, the Government mobilized the Army.

65

'Right! This time, when I shout: "Sewage stand-by squad, halt!" there's no need to stamp your feet.' *25 January 1983*

66 I've included this particular cartoon about the nuclear disaster at Chernobyl because soon after it appeared I had a phone-call from that wonderful gentleman, Phil Drabble, from TV's 'One Man and His Dog', and was very flattered when he asked for the original.

'I don't care what the Ministry of Agriculture says, the sheep haven't been the same since Chernobyl...'
24 June 1986

A brand-new £300,000 home was blown up in a village at war with developers.

'Tonight, ladies, Miss Truscott will give some useful tips on marmalade-making and how to keep houses off our green belt-areas...' *26 August 1988*

68 Health-inspectors who descended on the kitchens of the Dorchester Hotel discovered one ingredient that was not on the menu...cockroaches.

'Oh dear, I thought they'd got rid of the cockroaches...' *24 November 1988*

The scare over food-poisoning in eggs plunged MP Edwina Currie into a furious row. The Junior Health Minister was accused of deepening the crisis, threatening the industry and thousands of farming jobs.

'On second thoughts, Edwina, I'll just have toast.' *6 December 1988*

70 Firms were banned from using harmful CFC gases in British-made fridges in a campaign to get rid of the coolants which threaten to damage the atmosphere and expose people to harmful rays from the sun.

'By the way, I've chucked out the old fridge – it was unhygienic and destroying the ozone layer.'

3 March 1989

'Strewth, Sid – egg sandwiches! Are you sure that's wise?' *10 March 1989*

A black wave of death swept along the Alaskan coastline after the tanker *Exxon Valdez* was wrecked. Five days after the worst oil-spill in American history, scientists and fishermen were forced to accept that it was out of control. (This drawing harks back to a famous wartime cartoon by Philip Zec.)

The Price of Petrol is Going Up Again . . . *30 March 1989*

A Department of the Environment inquiry was launched after millions of gallons of untreated water were pumped into homes in the Rickmansworth area of Hertfordshire following a breakdown at the Three Valleys Water Services company.

'The water company says it's all right as long as you don't drink it...' *22 July 1991*

After 35 years of experiment, a research team in Oxford succeeded in creating energy by nuclear fusion, the same reaction that takes place in the heart of the sun.

'Why couldn't you have been a nuclear scientist? Doreen's husband has harnessed the power of the sun.'
12 November 1991

FOREIGN AFFAIRS

America's President Nixon had received a subpoena to appear before the Watergate Inquiry. Would he go to jail? Not a chance, but we all speculated. Judging by the style of the figure in the foreground I must have been very influenced by Ronald Searle at this time.

'Aw...C'mon, Clancy, tell us – who're you expectin' in?' *3 May 1973*

In the 1970s, Uganda's military dictator, Idi Amin, was a boon to cartoonists – as were nutty researchers. Someone conducting a survey on childhood intelligence came up with the theory that the tightness of a father's underpants could affect his offspring's IQ.

'Now, Mr Amin – before your little Idi was born, can you remember how tight your underpants were?' *8 November 1974*

Not for the first time the Government announced savage defence cuts – when trying to think of a new idea to fit a familiar story, the then current antics of the ever-confident fanatic General Amin seemed custom-made.

'It's Idi Amin! He must've heard about our defence cuts.' *5 December 1974*

Had the French conducted a nuclear test? America's President Jimmy Carter was
not too sure...

79

'*Mon Dieu*, Carter! Your American scientists are so sceptical...now listen closely – we are about to test anuzzer one.' *21 April 1978*

A row over alleged spying led to a wave of tit-for-tat expulsions of British
Embassy staff in Moscow and their Soviet counterparts in London.

'Just make enough for yourself Perkins – you've just become British Ambassador.' *16 September 1985*

After twenty-seven years in prison, African National Congress leader Nelson Mandela walked to freedom on 11 February 1990.

81

'After 27 years it's lovely having a man about the house again, Nelson.' *13 February 1990*

As statues were pulled down in the Soviet Republics, Britain's own symbols of Communism began to totter. *Morning Star* sales slumped to 10,000 copies a week and there were fears for Marx's bronze bust in Highgate Cemetery, London.

'I don't care if anyone does desecrate it! Take it back to Highgate Cemetery now!' *27 August 1991*

American President George Bush put pressure on Israeli PM Yitzhak Shamir to accept a land-for-peace initiative regarding the Israeli-occupied territories of Gaza, the Golan Heights and the West Bank.

'I think we're getting somewhere, Yitzhak. They say they worship the ground you walk on...'

1 November 1991

84 John Major's performance at the EU Conference in Maastricht was praised by
most Tories but was received with less enthusiasm elsewhere, some critics
drawing parallels with Neville Chamberlain's return from Munich.

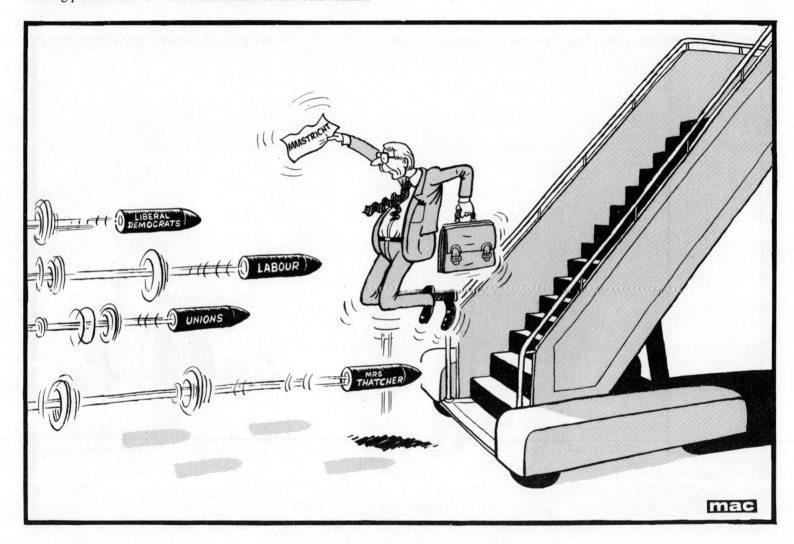

Peace In Our Time *12 December 1991*

During the US elections, outgoing Republican President Bush campaigned positively right up to the last minute, despite a massive surge in favour of Democrat Bill Clinton.

'Shucks, Dan, I guess all we can do now is wait – but I'm quietly confident...' *3 November 1992*

British Fisheries Protection Officers were kidnapped whilst attempting to confiscate equipment on board a French trawler caught fishing illegally off the Channel Islands.

'*Sacre bleu*, Papa! You spoil me. Two kilos of cod and a Fisheries Protection Officer.' *30 March 1993*

GREAT SPORTING MOMENTS

Romania's Ilie Nastase and America's Jimmy Connors were the stars of the Centre Court at Wimbledon in 1975 – not so much for their tennis as for their clowning. We could do with their like again – it all seems to be far too serious these days.

'A joke's a joke, Mr Nastase, but if you haven't put me and my chair back in five minutes...!' *26 June 1975*

'That's the sign of a great player – always chalks his cue before beating his opponent over the head with it.' *11 May 1978*

Scotland were knocked out of the 1978 football World Cup by Peru.

'Och, Hamish! I said it's the man from the Pru – not Peru!' *5 June 1978*

'If I hear you say "Whoopee, the glorious 12th!" just once more, Smithers, you'll be the first grouse flown to the Savoy!' *12 August 1985*

'From what I can gather, we appear to have won some vulgar football cup or something...' *16 May 1988*

**'Before "Match of the Day" can commence you are required to wave your football identity cards out of the
window in the direction of our TV satellite...'** *11 November 1988*

An ultra-sonic binocular-gun was 'the perfect way of nobbling racehorses', a court was told.

'Of course they're just ordinary binoculars, sir, but could we have a look?' *2 November 1989*

A love mystery deepened after it was alleged that Rumanian gymnast, Nadia Comaneci, planned to marry a man who already had a wife and four young children.

'Honestly, darling! Nothing has happened between us – Nadia's never still long enough!' *5 December 1989*

The macho image of Australia's bronzed beach-boys had sand kicked in its face when a survey revealed that most 'surfies' aged between 16 and 35 preferred riding the big waves to having sex.

'This sex thing, Dad. You tried it once, didn't you? What's it like?' *31 January 1991*

'Hey, André. That stuff you use on your chest. Steffi wants to know if you kept it in an old shampoo bottle.'

25 June 1993

Captain Graham Gooch resigned after England's cricketers failed to recapture the Ashes, suffering their eighth defeat in nine tests.

'Forget Italian pioneers. Wait till you see what Henderson is working on for England.' *27 July 1993*

**BUSINESS
AS USUAL**

100 At the time this cartoon appeared the country seemed to be permanently afflicted by strikes and stoppages, especially in the motor industry. This drawing, I was pleased to hear, was publicly torn to shreds by an irate union official in front of a gathering of strikers at a famous car factory.

'What's he got that we haven't?' *4 November 1975*

I've never been a great fan of Arthur Scargill and no doubt he doesn't think a lot of me. But I'd like to thank him now for constantly creating a deep mine for us cartoonists to work, by his never-ending outbursts, so loud in the 1970s and '80s, and with the occasional whimper today.

'Have a nice cup of tea and cheer up, Arthur – maybe you'll be able to bring down the Government next year.' *20 January 1982*

The Government proposed to scrap the curbs on Sunday trading and limited
opening hours, allowing customers to shop at any time on any day of the week...

'It's Mrs Mayhew again – ½lb. of streaky, a packet of Typhoo and she hasn't got all night...'
23 November 1984

Sir Ralph Halpern, chief executive of men's outfitters, the Burton Group, was involved in a sex scandal.

103

'Sir Ralph! We haven't reached "Any other business" yet!' *29 September 1987*

Marks & Spencer's were called in to show head teachers how to run their school budgets.

'Come on, come on! And the socks – I recognize British Home Stores socks!' *1 December 1988*

The Government's delight at the British Steel sell-off success was echoed by thousands of small investors who received in full the shares they had applied for.

105

'I don't care how many shares she bought. Get her out of here!' *5 December 1988*

106　A survey revealed that more than half Britain's executives drink to combat stress.
And the biggest cause of that worry among professionals and managers was
work, followed by money pressures and marriage problems.

'Today, gentlemen, the chairman's topic will be "Executive stress and drinking. Is it a myth?" '
21 February 1989

Having beaten France, England's hopes in the Rugby World Cup soared as they prepared to face Scotland in the semi-final. Meanwhile, the Judge Thomas sexual harassment case in America remained in the public eye.

'Ah, Mr Bumstrode. I was just demonstrating to your secretary a few tactics our gallant rugby lads might employ against the Scots next Saturday.' *21 October 1991*

Bank of England employee Christine Gibson was charged with stealing thousands of pounds of old notes smuggled out in her bra and knickers from the incinerator depot at the Bank's printing works in Debden, Essex.

'Perhaps it's spring, Miss Trimley. But before you go home the manager would like to take a peek inside your bra...' *15 April 1994*

Prime Minister John Major asked the public to report beggars to the police, angering campaigners for the homeless. Earlier in the year a professional beggar had been arrested after being caught driving a £10,000 L-registration car.

'Would you come back later? I'm seeing my accountant right now.' *15 September 1994*

110 Shell finally dropped plans to dump its 462-foot Brent Spar oil-platform in the Atlantic after protests from Greenpeace and European ministers over the leakage of toxic sludge. It was moored temporarily in a Norwegian fjord.

'Look at that, Kirsten. Washing-machines, old cars, rubbish...whatever next?' *22 June 1995*

**WARS AND
PEACE**

It was reported that the fugitive Nazi war criminal, Martin Bormann, had been found living in Argentina. This was just one of umpteen sightings. Perhaps the Nazis had perfected cloning. I have a theory that he and Lord Lucan are actually living in a squat in Cleethorpes.

'Martin Bormann? No – me Jane.' *21 March 1972*

Bernadette Devlin, always to be found at the heart of Republican protests and demonstrations in Northern Ireland at this time, got married. We all worried for the husband . . .

' 'Twas only a little tiff, Bernadette, darlin' – what's it goin' to be like if we have a real quarrel?'
25 April 1973

114

In 1974 Americans, quite rightly, were preoccupied with the wrongdoings of their President, Richard Nixon. They were a lot more forgiving, however, with some of their soldiers found guilty of atrocities in Vietnam.

'Hell, don't worry, son – anyone can make a mistake.' *27 September 1974*

Women demonstrated for peace in Ulster but the men of violence took no heed.

115

29 November 1976

After the Falklands War, Britain pressed the Argentinian ruling *junta* to officially declare a 'cessation to all hostilities' so that they could send prisoners of war home. Otherwise, they warned, there could be a 'major disaster relief problem' coping with the hundreds of POWs held in British camps.

'I hate to spoil the victory celebrations, but I think they've worked out how to feed those Argie POWs.' *17 June 1982*

There was considerable embarrassment in historical circles when it was discovered that diaries allegedly written by Adolf Hitler were in fact fakes.

'...WEDNESDAY...ANOTHER HOT DAY...' *27 April 1983*

118 What a sense of humour America's President Reagan must have had, threatening to 'nuke' Russia on air! He hadn't realized that the microphone was switched on when he declared 'I have just signed legislation which outlaws Russia. The bombing begins in five minutes.' How they must have laughed...

'Guess what, comrades? – it was just Reagan's little joke.' *15 August 1984*

'Of course, dear, after you've fixed the burst pipes, cleared the snow and reconnected the electricity, I'd love to hear what it was like being a hostage in Iraq.' *11 December 1990*

120 TV chiefs ignored floods of complaints about blanket coverage of the Gulf War disrupting regular programme schedules. Thames TV alone received 700 letters a day, mostly from fans of soap operas.

'...and now, another non-stop bombardment of repeat film-clips, analysis, news and views from the Gulf...'
25 January 1991

After 25 years of bloodshed in Ulster, the IRA announced a 'complete cessation of military operations' from midnight on 21 August 1994.

121

'After long and careful consideration...' *1 September 1994*

The VE-Day celebrations in Britain included nationwide street parties and a huge festival in Hyde Park featuring a Veterans' Centre equipped with a computer-linked search facility to help reunite old wartime comrades.

'Remind me, Albert. How did I sneak through the German lines in 1944?' *9 May 1995*

GETTING
THERE...

124

Looking back at the drawings I've done over the last 25 years, I'm amazed how much my style has changed. In this case the story was about the British Government's desperate bid to sell Concorde abroad. Without too much success as it turned out.

'Good grief, Your Highness – they cost *much* more assembled.' *6 June 1972*

Strikes, protest, demos. Joe Gormley, President of the National Union of Miners, was not the most popular man in the country at this time. 'Hurry up and retire,' we thought, things would get better then. Little did we know…

'That's right, sir – we've got the railway militants in the pipeline.' *19 February 1975*

As the railways were clogged up yet again in winter conditions (this was drawn
10 years before the infamous 'wrong type of snow' excuse), the short-lived
Advanced Passenger Train, which could tilt on corners, was launched.

**'My fault, really. I asked him, "How many more years before British Rail can cope with
a bit of snow?" – then he hit his tilt button.'** *9 December 1981*

A train-driver admitted that he was at home in bed when he should have been on duty. I was amazed by how many people sent me cut-outs of this cartoon with crosses where they thought the driver should be! Jokingly, I wrote to them saying they'd won a six-month-old British Rail sandwich. Later I got letters complaining that they hadn't received their prize . . .

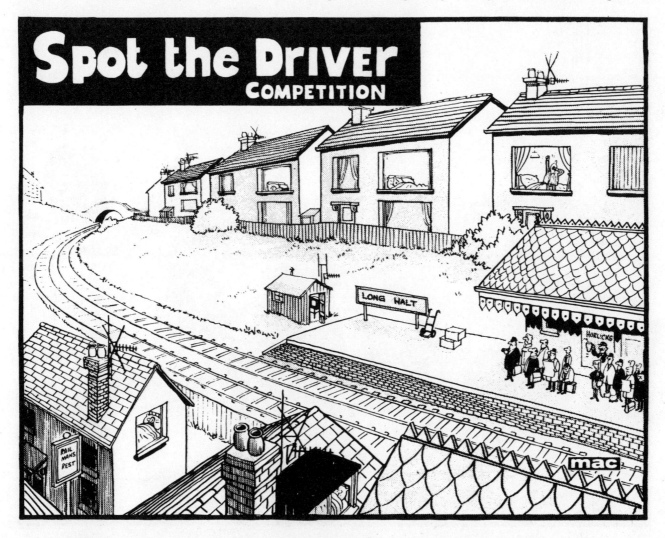

Place a cross where you think the exact centre of the driver is. *25 January 1982*

BR's cuts led to strikes by train-drivers and other rail workers on Southern Region's 'misery line'. Commuters were not amused...

'Members of the jury, you have heard how the accused dragged the train-driver from his cab, beat him, set fire to his trousers and made him swallow a railway timetable...do you find him guilty or not guilty?' *2 February 1982*

'**Oh good! It looks as though they've been having lovely weather in Greece.'** *10 August 1987*

130 The Department of the Environment introduced National Lead Free Petrol week
in an attempt to promote 'greener' fuels.

'Unleaded? You're in luck, zur, there be a garage sells that new-fangled stuff 20 miles up the road...'
3 November 1988

'British Rail is pleased to announce the re-opening of the Great Twissington-on-Crouch railway station – your next train is due in approximately...' *1 August 1991*

132   After years of debate, Transport Secretary John MacGregor finally decided on the route the Channel Tunnel link-line would take through Kent, terminating at St Pancras.

'Good news! The Channel Tunnel rail-link isn't coming this way after all.' *23 March 1993*

A new advertising campaign in BR's Network Southeast region suggested that stress-free rail travel left commuters more energy to devote to their sex lives.

'I'm sorry, Cynthia. There's just a certain something about the way Raymond punches my ticket in the mornings...' *16 July 1993*

The Council for the Protection of Rural England announced that 27,500 acres of countryside are lost to urban planners and roadbuilders each year, despite a stable population.

'Do you realize that 27,500 acres of countryside are disappearing under concrete every year in England?'
30 July 1993

PARLIAMENTARY PRACTICES

The Tory Government was at a low ebb in 1974 and there were rumours that Prime Minister Ted Heath might resign. The drawing of the flying figure is a conscious tribute to the caricature of former Tory premier Harold Macmillan as 'Supermac', created by the *Evening Standard*'s cartoonist Vicky.

'Let's see now – if Heath resigns, there's Whitelaw, Du Cann, Thatcher, Joseph – who else could rescue the party?' *14 October 1974*

At a State Opening of Parliament during Harold Wilson's premiership, the papers were full of stories about the Labour PM's business affairs. Was this a smear campaign? Mysteriously his income-tax papers disappeared...

'... and my total earnings for 1973-4 were ... oh, dear, I seem to have someone's tax forms mixed up with my speech.' *27 October 1974*

In the election for a new Conservative leader, Ted Heath was toppled and Margaret Thatcher became the first woman ever to lead a political party in Britain. Her stepping-stones are (right to left): Heath, Howe, Du Cann, Prior and Whitelaw.

One Small Step for Woman – A Giant Leap for Womankind. *12 February 1975*

Prime Minister Harold Wilson suddenly resigned – leaving the Labour Party, the nation and the press in a frenzy of speculation as to who would replace him. I racked my brains for an idea and happily remembered it was 1 April.

'Hurry up, Harold – I'm dying to see their faces when you tear up your resignation and say "APRIL FOOL".' *1 April 1976*

As Mrs Thatcher prepared for her high-pressure visit to Moscow, it was announced that a cure had been found for baldness.

'Before I go to Moscow, Denis, have you seen anything of my blood-pressure tablets?' *24 March 1987*

'You'd think he would've told her what he was putting in his Budget, wouldn't you?' *14 March 1988*

142 In 1989, with the railways, docks and town halls already on strike, Arthur Scargill planned to add to Britain's worst summer of strife for 15 years by bringing out the miners over a pay claim.

'It's all right, Denis. Mr Heath is explaining how he dealt with a glut of strikes back in 1974...' *10 July 1989*

In a sensational turnround, Margaret Thatcher, the longest-serving Prime Minister this century, resigned. Foreign Secretary Douglas Hurd and Chancellor John Major threw their hats into the ring.

Who's Big Enough? *23 November 1990*

Neil Kinnock fired his electoral starting-gun by stating that under Labour there would be no tax-cuts for five years and that the National Insurance contributions ceiling would be abolished. Had he shot himself in the foot?

'...and furthermore, we'll bleed you dry – you fat, go-getting, wealth-creating git!...I do hope we can count on your support.' *10 May 1991*

Tory sex scandals continued with the bizarre death of Stephen Milligan and the resignation of Hartley Booth, Mrs Thatcher's successor as MP for Finchley. Munch's *The Scream* was stolen from Oslo's National Gallery.

The Scream *14 February 1994*

146 Manchester United footballer, Eric Cantona, was fined and suspended when he violently attacked an abusive spectator in a match against Crystal Palace. Former Prime Minister, Edward Heath, had similar feelings about John Major's policies at the time.

'I think Ted's been watching too much football.' *30 January 1995*

A LITTLE GALLIMAUFRY

'Nosey, nosey, Mother-in-law... that was meant to be a surprise for tomorrow!'
11 March 1972

This was a lovely story – should women in the services be armed? Some folks claimed I was being sexist. Was I? Whatever. It was only meant to be a bit of fun.

'Mavis thought she saw a mouse!' *14 March 1979*

150

The whole nation was shocked when Eric Morecambe died. He was one of the funniest and best-loved comedians of this century. This drawing was reproduced on the programme for his memorial service.

You brought us sunshine, you brought us laughter, you brought us love... *29 May 1984*

'I've waited till I'm eighty and you have a headache?' *27 July 1984*

152 Britain most definitely is a nation of dog-lovers. I am one myself (my little West Highland terrier appears here). I'd like to think that heaven does have a place for dogs and that perhaps that wonderful lady, Barbara Woodhouse – who died in 1988 – is keeping them all in order.

'It was heaven. Rolling in dirt, barking and fighting and doing as we pleased – then Barbara Woodhouse came up...' *11 July 1988*

Women are climbing the ladder of home improvement, a survey reported. They have been joining the DIY brigade because many hard-up couples just cannot afford professional help for work in the home.

'Can she ring you later? I don't like to disturb her while she's doing her housework.' *7 March 1989*

154   American pop-star, Madonna, launched her new film-production company and
caused a shudder in the Brontë Society when she revealed that she was
considering playing the role of Cathy in a remake of *Wuthering Heights*.

'Madonna, honey – you shout: "Heathcliff, Heathcliff." Then run into his arms – GENTLY!' *1 May 1992*

Two 19-year-old girl students at Norlands Nursery Training College in Hungerford, Britain's top school for nannies, were expelled after it was revealed that they had taken the drug Ecstasy at 'rave' parties.

'Please, Rupert. Don't jump to conclusions about the new nanny – after all, Mary Poppins used to do that.'
17 November 1992

156 When two 10-year-old boys were charged with the murder of a toddler abducted whilst shopping with his parents in Bootle, Lancashire, the Government promised a blitz on teenage crime.

'This one's a bit far-fetched. A kid who has to call his teacher "Sir" nicks something, gets a thick ear from a copper and is sent home to find his employed parents are in and not at the pub...' *22 February 1993*

After a public outcry against a spate of six-figure compensations to sacked pregnant servicewomen, former Women's Royal Army Corps Lieutenant Lesley Disney received £7,000 from an Employment Appeals Tribunal in Exeter.

'... and what do I get for producing you, you 'orrible little man? – The sack and a measly £7,000 compensation. STAND TO ATTENTION WHEN I'M TALKING TO YOU!' *8 September 1994*

Popular TV game-show host Michael Barrymore split from his wife and admitted to having been gay for many years.

'Who'd have thought it – Michael Barrymore living a lie for 19 years?' *25 August 1995*

ACKNOWLEDGEMENTS

First and foremost I would like to thank Sir David English, Paul Dacre and also all the Deputy Editors of the *Daily Mail* who, over the years, have sifted through my drawings and sorted out the wheat from the chaff. Thanks too to the ever-helpful staff working in the Associated Newspapers' Photo Services Department and Picture Library, and to all my friends, past and present, on the Art Desk.

To my wife Janet, who has helped and encouraged me for the past decade and a half, and to Maureen, who was such a wonderful support in the early years, must go a special debt of gratitude. Thanks too to Nick Spargo, who taught me all I know, and to Glyn Walker, my childhood pal, whose enthusiasm and dexterity with a pencil first fired my desire to draw. And last but not least, many thanks to Mark Bryant, who in an insane moment thought that this book would be a good idea, to Deirdre McDonald without whom all his good ideas would probably have come to nothing, and to designer Mick Keates who turned 25 years of dusty drawings into such an attractive volume.

STAN McMURTRY, better known as MAC, was born in Edinburgh on 4 May 1936. He moved to Birmingham at the age of eight, studied at Birmingham College of Art and spent his National Service in the Royal Army Ordnance Corps. At first he worked as a cartoon animator, helping to produce films for ITV (two of which won awards at Cannes Film Festivals), and became a freelance cartoonist in 1965.

He joined the Daily Sketch *as Political and Social Cartoonist in 1969 and moved to the* Daily Mail *in 1971. He has also contributed joke cartoons (as Stan McMurtry) to* Punch *and other publications, worked in advertising, illustrated books, designed greetings cards and written comedy scripts for Dave Allen and Tommy Cooper. As well as his bestselling* MAC's Year *annuals (first published in 1975), he has also produced a children's book,* The Bunjee Venture, *which was made into a cartoon film by Hanna Barbera.*

Twice voted Social and Political Cartoonist of the Year by the Cartoonists' Club of Great Britain (and twice as overall Cartoonist of the Year), he has also been voted Man of the Year by RADAR.